The Extraordinary Gift: Our Teachers

By Janet Pilcher and Quint Studer

Published by Studer Education

Pensacola, Florida
Denver, Colorado

First Edition

2025

ISBN: 978-1-7371170-2-5

books@studereducation.com

Studer Education
Attn: Book Department
6732 W Coal Mine Ave, Unit 501
Littleton, CO 80123

To learn more about Studer Education, visit us online:

www.StuderEducation.com

Expressing My Gratitude

I would like to extend my deepest appreciation to several people who made this book possible.

First, I am honored to have written this book with Quint Studer. He is a mentor and friend who matters to so many people. I am grateful to him for giving me an opportunity to position education as one of the most coveted and valued professions. He is a masterful teacher himself, and it is through his teachings that I have grown to understand that leadership is about helping people know they matter, and he has spent time with me to reinforce my value to him. He has even taken me on several road trips to be onsite with healthcare leaders, allowing me to learn from those experiences. He has taught me, guided me, and cared for me. He has helped me see that I matter. Quint is an extraordinary gift to me and to many others.

Thank you, Barbara Scott, for being a support to Quint and helping us get this book together. We can always count on you.

Thank you to the teachers who are honored in this book. Their stories are powerful and real. You are the true difference makers. Your memory will live forever in the lives you touch.

Thank you to the following individuals who contributed to telling the stories in this book. This work would not be possible without you.

- Monica Woods, thank you for engaging in an interview with Holly and me to share insights about Mr. Gulley's impact on your life.
- Dr. Charlotte Boling, thank you for having the courage to share your story with the world.
- Dr. KK Owen and Dr. Gayle Juneau-Butler, thank you for working together to share the selfless story of Ms. Enga McClendon.
- Dr. Pat Greco, thank you for doing interviews and sharing the stories of Ms. Erin Brodzeller and Ms. Robbie Fackelman. You've seen many teachers along the way. We are grateful that you chose to share the stories of these two teachers who were called to their path to impact others.
- Dr. Robin Largue, thank you for opening us to the world of Ms. Tiana Walker through your volunteer work as a Pre-K Reading Pal. Ms. Walker shows us the power of children having a Pre-K educational experience.
- Superintendent Kevin Case, thank you for your partnership and allowing us to share the story of Francis Case Elementary School's recognition program. Thank you, Principal Clark and Ms. Finney, for engaging in a conversation with Holly and me so we could tell your story. It's one that so many of us can learn from and act on. Thank you to one of the district's leader coaches, Dr. Casey Blochowiak, for sharing the story with us.

Thank you to Deborah McIntyre who works alongside me in every step of my journey, encouraging me and focusing me on completing works like this one.

Thank you, Ashley Storey, for being the Accelerate Your Performance Podcast producer and helping me tell purposeful stories every Monday about the bright spots in education.

And a huge thank you to Dr. Holly Ellis. Holly is the person who works as my co-developer of creative writings and solutions. Holly started years ago as my graduate assistant at the University of West Florida. I had the opportunity several years back to recruit Holly to work with me as we advanced our work and reach at Studer Education. She is my lifeline for accomplishing work that I believe can make a difference in our profession. I couldn't do what I do without her. Holly is a kind, giving, and selfless person who makes a tremendous difference in my life.

Finally, I extend my deepest appreciation to David Marshall. On January 1st, 2025, David's long-term passion for our work at Studer Education led him to acquire our organization and partner with me so that we can extend our reach to K12 school districts and higher education institutions throughout the world. David has been one of my best colleagues over the years as he has helped me design a vision, execute that vision, build connections of our work, and stay true to our core mission of creating great places for students to learn, faculty to teach, staff to work, and families to send their children to be successful. David is a talented entrepreneur who is driven by his passion for doing good in the world. He is the designer of the cover and layout of this book. I am grateful to David for being a partner to our team to make a difference in the lives of others.

Janet Pilcher

Table of Contents

Foreword

By Quint Studer

I speak at many conferences and in front of large groups. They're usually businesspeople, healthcare leaders, physicians, and others. One question I always ask is this: When you think about your own life and career, can you remember a teacher (or teachers) who had a huge impact on your life?

I've been asking this question for years with thousands and thousands of people, and I've never had anyone not raise their hand. Everyone can remember someone who made a difference. We then share stories about those impactful teachers – from preschool all the way through college.

I follow up by asking, "Have you had the chance to thank that person?" And while most people would love to, the reality is that many never have. That's certainly true in my case with Mrs. James, Mr. Frye, and Coach King, who had a profound influence on me.

Some people do find a way to say "thank you," but for others, life happens. Sometimes they can't locate the person anymore, or maybe the educator has passed on. Still, the lack of a formal "thank you" doesn't diminish the impact those people had. That's a big part of why I've remained so committed to helping those in education not to underestimate the impact they have made and make. It's out of deep respect and awe for those who do this work.

Let me go back to my own story.

I was born in a suburb of Chicago called Berwyn at MacNeal Hospital. My first school was Congress Park Elementary in Brookfield, Illinois. I don't remember much about kindergarten, first grade, or second grade. I only remember fragments from photos, but I vividly remember third grade.

Third grade was pivotal for me, and I only made it there because my mom lobbied for it. Kindergarten through second grade was tough. I had a speech impediment, and while the school offered speech therapy, which I was grateful for, being pulled out of class made me feel different. Reintegration was always awkward. On top of that, I really struggled with reading.

If you read my second-grade report card, the third-quarter comment from Mrs. Snyder says: "Based on Quint's reading at this point, we suggest he repeat second grade." My mom was already worried about how I felt about myself, and she feared what repeating a grade might do to my self-esteem. Teacher conferences were always tough for her, not because she didn't care, but because she rarely heard anything that was positive or made her feel hopeful. My mom and the school reached a compromise: I would be passed into third grade on a six-week trial.

I'm sure my mom worked hard with me at home, but the person who truly changed my life was Mrs. James, my third-grade teacher. I don't know what degrees or certifications she had, but what I do know is that she made me feel safe and loved. She had this remarkable ability to wrap her arms around you – even when she wasn't physically doing it.

She never called on me to read aloud if she thought it would make me uncomfortable or set me up to fail. Instead, she put me in positions to succeed. She also knew that motivation matters, especially in reading. Since I loved sports, she'd bring in the Chicago Tribune sports section, and we'd go through it together. She pulled out words from sports stories and taught me how to read using something I was passionate about. I didn't realize it at the time, but that's exactly what she was doing – building my literacy through sports reporting.

That passion also helped me with math. If you love sports, you need to understand stats – batting averages, points per game, and so on. Mrs. James helped me thrive without ever making me feel small.

She even gave me a speaking part in a school play. For a kid with a speech impediment, that was terrifying but also empowering. My line was "I'm as poor as ever." She told me to think of pouring milk when I said the word "poor." To this day, I still remember that line, and I remember exactly where my mom sat during that play: second row from the windows, third seat.

That moment mattered so much because my mom got to see her son, who she thought might never speak clearly, perform in front of a classroom. I only ever showed up late to third grade once, and it was because I had picked some irises on the way back from lunch to give to Mrs. James.

That was third grade, and while every teacher matters, some leave a lifelong imprint.

Another major influence in my life was Mr. Frye, my sixth-grade teacher at Seventh Avenue School in La Grange, Illinois. Mr. Frye liked me, and I could feel it. I struggled academically with both speech and hearing challenges. Mr. Frye understood that, so he placed my desk close to his (maybe the closest in the room). It let him help me subtly, without making it obvious to others. He shared with my mother that I had a lot of energy, and it needed to be channeled in the right direction.

He'd involve me in little tasks (like grading papers and running errands) both to keep me engaged and to protect me from feeling left out or distracted. Again, he found ways to support me without embarrassing me.

I loved sports, but, unfortunately, I wasn't great at them. In middle school, I tried out for the basketball team, and I was certain the NBA was in my future. That dream died quickly when I didn't make the seventh-grade team, but Mr. Frye stepped in. He invited me back to referee the fifth- and sixth-grade games. That small act kept me connected and gave me a sense of purpose.

Later, I attended Lyons Township High School in La Grange, one of the biggest high schools in Illinois. I still loved sports and wanted to participate. The school offered cross country and football. Cross country wasn't for me; I ran around the block once and was done. And football? I was under 100 pounds as a freshman, so that wasn't happening, either.

Then, a friend told me they were starting a new sport: soccer. I didn't know much about it except what I saw on Channel 26, a Spanish-language station in Chicago. But it involved a ball, and that was enough for me. I tried out, and that's when I met another difference-maker: Coach John King.

Coach King never cut anyone…maybe because it was our first year. He had a way of correcting you without making you feel bad. He knew I was a sensitive kid who wouldn't respond well to "tough love," but I would respond to love. Once at soccer practice, I went to kick the ball and missed, and he said, "Good effort getting to the ball. Next time, put your foot out there."

Coach King had a gift for lifting people up, and he would go on to play a pivotal role in my life. I'll share more about that as the story continues.

Coach King had the ability to make someone feel good. My freshman and sophomore years, I played on the freshman-sophomore team. He played me for one half in each game. I felt like I was part of the team. It's nice, when you're not doing well academically, to have an outlet where you feel a part *of* something, not apart *from* it.

My junior year, things got more difficult. I went out for soccer, and very quickly I was cut. There were two people cut right off the bat, and I was one of those two. So, there I was, a junior in high school, not doing well academically, cut from a soccer team that, for the first time ever, cut people, and I just didn't know what to do. I plundered through my junior year of high school. Then, my senior year came. Soccer always started a couple of weeks before school started, and I didn't try out for the soccer team (of course) because I'd been cut the year before. I got a phone call from Lee Benasek, who was on the soccer team. I've known Lee since elementary school, and Lee called me and said, "Hey, Quint, Coach King wants to know why you're not out for soccer."

I was really confused, and I said, "Well, Lee, he's the freshman-sophomore coach." Lee responded, "No, he's the new varsity coach. He wants me to call you and tell you to come out." (I get emotional just telling this story.)

I went out for soccer my senior year, and Coach King told us when we were going to play regardless of whether we were winning or losing. I always knew, though, that I was going to get to play. Back then, soccer games included four quarters, and I usually played in the first and third quarters. Just knowing that I would get to play made the difference for me.

I also had two study halls. If you had two study halls, during one of the study halls, you could do other things, such as go lift weights or go to the library.

Coach King had me come to his special education classroom during one of my study halls to be his student assistant. My goal as a student assistant was to help him with his students. I also would walk them to the library. We'd leave the classroom to go to the library a little after the bell rang, and we'd head back to the classroom before the bell rang because the students at the time would sometimes be teased in the hallways. Today it's so much different, but back then, well, maybe it's not different, but back then they'd hear hurtful words like "retard" and "spec-ed." I had great empathy for those kids. I could relate to them and how they felt.

I graduated from high school, and I did pretty well on the ACT test. My parents and I went to Wisconsin during the summer, and there was a school there called Whitewater. So, I went to Wisconsin and attended the University of Wisconsin-Whitewater.

My dad hadn't gone to college, and my mom hadn't gone to college. Really, very few people in our family had ever gone to college. Because I didn't know what to major in, I majored in "undecided." I needed 120 credits to graduate, and I took 60 credits of "undecided." At the end of my sophomore year, I met with the school counselor at Whitewater, and he explained to me that I had pretty much taken most of the courses that could be taken as an undecided major. I needed to select a major. Otherwise, I might take courses that wouldn't count toward my graduation. I had to graduate in four years. He asked me what I thought I would like to major in.

I thought of teaching because teachers had made a huge impact on my life, particularly Mrs. James, Mr. Fry, and Coach King. Then my advisor said, “What age would you like to teach?” Well, I loved sports, so I thought of high school because I believed the pep rallies, sports, and fanfare would be fun. I loved the whole feeling of it.

Then he said, “Well, what would you like to teach in high school?” Again, not being a great student, I was worried because I can't spell. How can you be a teacher and go up to the blackboard to write if you can’t spell? But I remembered what Coach King did.

I explained to my counselor what I had done at Lyons Township High School with Coach King. When I finished, he said, “You want to be a special education teacher.” So, I became a special education teacher.

Once again, I was very fortunate. Whitewater had a Special Education Department, and when you walked in, the first person you saw was Florence Kopas, and she was wonderful. In fact, my wife and I donated money to have a room named after her at the University of Wisconsin-Whitewater. Her husband was a farmer in Jefferson, and she worked as an administrative assistant. Once you walked in the department, Mrs. Kopas made you feel loved.

Along with Mrs. Kopas, I was lucky to encounter Dr. Thiede, Dr. Hahn, Dr. Lauritzen, and Dr. Pease, people who made me feel that I was loved and that I belonged. With their help, I became a teacher. Behind every teacher is often another teacher who once made them feel seen, loved, or inspired. I had teachers who did just that for me, and I wanted to do that for others.

I was very fortunate that I was able to help place children with special needs or special abilities in jobs. I worked for an organization called CESA at the time, Cooperative Educational Service Agency, in Rock County, Wisconsin, trying to help students get jobs. I was the person that worked in summer programs for the school district and for regional service providers to help place students with jobs.

Now, I own a minor league baseball team in Pensacola, Florida, called the Pensacola Blue Wahoos. If you ever come to one of our games, you'll realize that we're one big vocational training organization. It's just magic when you walk up the stairs. First, they're alphabetized, color-coded, and numbered, so we can teach as people come to a game. You then see Tea at the top of the stairs, who's in a wheelchair and is not overly verbal, but if you just say, "Thank you for working today, Tea," and are patient, she'll say, "Thank you for having me."

I'm a big proponent of teachers and the impact they make. Once a student is helped to achieve, doors are opened. No matter who a student is, where they come from, who their family is, or what interests they have, teachers make a huge impact, and that impact extends from students in a classroom to adults in the "real world."

That's why it has been so important to me to help teachers feel recognized and supported, which is why I have worked with Dr. Janet Pilcher. Our goal is to create cultures where people feel valued, feel joy, and say, "I can't imagine doing anything else." I have immense gratitude for teachers.

Education is different from most organizations, companies, and industries. I've worked in healthcare for many years. When I give a keynote or a talk, almost immediately afterward and even during breaks, people clap, come up to me, and tell me how much they enjoyed it. In healthcare (not that it's an easy profession by any means), you often get recognized right away for doing good work.

You've all experienced it: you take your child to the emergency department, and after receiving care, you say, "thank you." You thank the doctor. You thank the nurse. A friend of mine, Marv, was recently in a bad accident. His wife was texting me regularly, and she also reached out to the hospital president to thank them for the excellent care Marv received at Ascension Sacred Heart in Pensacola, Florida.

What I'm saying is this: in most professions, appreciation is immediate. At the Pensacola Blue Wahoos games, for instance, the ushers often get a "thank you" right away. When you go to a restaurant and receive good service, you say, "thank you." In almost every industry, the people providing the service or product hear their "thank you" right then and there.

Now imagine this: I give a talk, people enjoy it, but I hear nothing. Twenty-two years later, I get a note that says, "You really made a difference when you spoke." That's the kind of delayed appreciation that teachers and others in the classroom often experience, and I think that's tough. Even if they intellectually understand the impact they make, the emotional delay in appreciation is hard.

I once spoke in North Carolina at a healthcare system. Before the talk, they had asked me to make sure I told the story about Coach King. When I finished the story, Coach King walked onto the stage. They had flown him to North Carolina to be in the audience. That day, I was able to express to Coach King the immense gratitude I felt for the impact he had on my life.

If I were a principal, one thing I'd do is take an hour every day just to call parents. Often, when parents get a call from the school, their first thought is, "Uh-oh, what's wrong?" What if we flipped that? What if we were proactive and called to say, "I just want to let you know how much your child's teacher appreciates them," or "Your child did something wonderful today"? I think 99% of the time, the parent would then say something positive about the teacher in return.

That's why, when Janet and her team teach the concept of rounding, they emphasize that when someone from administration walks into a classroom, the teacher should feel good. They should think, "Oh great! Here comes something positive." Maybe they're bringing a note from a parent, saying how much they appreciate the difference that teacher is making in their child's life.

I shared earlier that when I speak around the country, I often ask, "Have any of you had a teacher who made a difference in your life?" Every hand goes up. I give them time to share, and the stories are powerful. I heard one recently from a chief nurse executive. She grew up in a very poor area. Her family had very little money, but someone at her school made her feel special and told her, "I think you'd make a great nurse." They helped her get into school, and now she leads an entire hospital nursing staff.

These are the kinds of differences teachers make. It's not just teachers; it is aides, custodians, bus drivers, and everyone else in the school ecosystem who can be a difference-maker. Sometimes, the bus driver is the first person a child sees in the morning. If that bus driver greets the child warmly and makes them feel seen, it can change the entire trajectory of that child's day.

That's what this book is about. It's not just a book for educators and school staff to read; it's also for non-educators. We want people to read it and then pass this gift along – to a teacher, a principal, a bus driver, or anyone else – with a simple message:

Thank you.

Thank you for what you do.

Thank you for making a difference in my child's life.

Thank you for the impact you make in the lives of so many children.

This is a book of appreciation. It's a passage of love. It's about helping those who make such a meaningful difference in our lives feel seen, valued, and deeply appreciated. The work they do has purpose. It's worthwhile, and it changes lives over and over again.

THANK YOU NOTE

Dear Ms. James, Mr. Frye, and Coach King,

You made a difference in my life. I speak to many audiences and tell the story of how you cared for me. I am grateful for how each of you helped me.

Ms. James – thank you for making me feel loved and special. Your care for me gave me confidence that I could succeed.

Mr. Frye – thank you for channeling my energy and liking me. I felt that every day in your class, and I still remember that feeling.

Coach King – thank you for giving me an opportunity to play a sport, the one thing in life I loved the most but was not very good at. Thank you for giving me the opportunity to work with you and your special education class when I was a high school student. It led to me deciding to become a special education teacher.

To all of you – your interactions with me have had a wide-reaching and lasting impact. Through your stories, your reach extends to others. Thank you for making a difference in my life so that I can make a difference in the lives of others.

I am grateful,

Quint

Quint Studer

Introduction

Quint and I both live in Pensacola, so we have had the opportunity to work collaboratively on numerous projects, and we are honored to work on this book together.

While I was the dean of the College of Professional Studies at The University of West Florida, I learned about Quint because of the tremendous contributions he made in our community, and I wanted to be part of that impact. His accomplishments leading healthcare organizations moved him to start Studer Group, a healthcare leadership coaching company. He and his team were advancing healthcare organizations to become great places for people to work and serve patients with "best in class" customer service.

I was excited when I had the opportunity to connect with Quint. When we first met, he told me the story about the three teachers summarized in the foreword of this book. He also invited me to be a guest at his company's quarterly professional development sessions and the Studer Group conferences that occurred throughout the year where he presented. I attended as many conferences as I could, and Quint made it possible for me to do so. I listened to some of the material repeatedly, taking notes and learning something each time.

From those experiences and my interactions with Quint, I have learned that the most important job of a leader is to show people you value them and to demonstrate how they add value. Since that time, I've been committed to developing my skills to lead with this awesome responsibility, and I am humbled every day by how difficult leading is and how important it is to always be a student of leadership.

My leadership experiences have taken me on a journey. In 2010, I left a secure position as a tenured, full professor and key leader at the university level to take Quint's practices in healthcare and transfer those to education. Quint opened the door for me to make this courageous decision. I remember on my first day of the job, I met with Quint to ask him what he wanted me to do. He tore off a piece of paper and wrote, "Janet Pilcher can do what Janet Pilcher does best." He believed in me, he knew I mattered, and he knew that I would grow Studer Education in a way that shows others they are valued and how they are of value to others. I still have Quint's note. When times get tough, I pull it out and read it to remember that I matter.

Now, I have the opportunity every day to share that message with others and show them that they matter. I am fortunate to work alongside people who make a difference, educators who touch lives and change students' lives – be it teachers, bus drivers, cafeteria workers, custodians, principals, or district leaders.

Every person who works in a school system is an educator, and they show up to work every day wanting to give their best to students. This book is a gift to all of you who make a difference in the lives of others through your passion, dedication, and drive to help students live to their human potential. You are an extraordinary gift to our world.

When we say, "you are a gift," we express our admiration and appreciation for the value you bring to others. You change the lives of those you touch. That is a remarkable and awesome responsibility that you assume every day. Simply put, you matter.

Dr. Zach Mercurio (a researcher, author, professor, and strategist) suggests that "mattering" is the belief that we are significant in the world. Feeling like we matter depends on being valued by others and adding value to others. We **feel valued** when people know our name, ask about our life, know what our struggles are, remember what's important to us, and check on how we are doing. We feel we **add value** when people show us how we make a difference, affirm our unique talents and gifts, ask for our opinion, give us responsibility, and rely on us. We need to tell others when they add value to our lives; they need to hear our stories of value.

There are so many teachers, staff, and leaders who are creating meaningful stories every day – millions of them that are seldom told. Therefore, in this book, we focus on telling teacher stories. *The Extraordinary Gift* is a way to honor and appreciate our teachers and educators; it is our way to honor the value of teachers. It's a way to share powerful acts of love and compassion that occur in our classrooms and schools across the world every minute of every day. These stories demonstrate the impact educators have on the lives of students, their families, and each other.

Following the stories, we share a chapter on ways to continue to keep this book alive. We offer actions we can all take to show our gratitude to those who are making a difference in the lives of students, families, and our communities.

So, this is a book for anyone. It's a book that some of us can relate to as teachers and educators and that others can connect with because of teachers who made a difference in their lives. We hope that after reading this book you take the stories of human kindness and make life better for others –

show people that you value them and how they add value to others. In turn, by doing so, you will make life better for you.

The stories in Chapters 1 to 8 are introduced by Janet. The first story in Chapter 1 is Janet's personal one about a teacher who made a difference in her life. The remainder of the stories highlighted in Chapters 2 to 8 were gathered through interviews and written narratives. These stories represent only a few of the millions to be told and recognized.

We hope you enjoy the stories as much as we did. They show why teachers and educators are indeed an extraordinary gift.

Chapter 1
The Story of Ms. Melrose Coleman

I, Janet, start the stories with one of my own. My education was important to my mom and dad. Going to college was simply my next path after high school. So, my job growing up was to travel this path. It is one that was influenced by my mom and dad and Ms. Melrose Coleman.

My dad was the youngest of an Alabama farming and small business family of five brothers and two sisters who eventually moved to Pace, Florida, to run a small store. Dad and his four brothers were barbers in Pensacola, Florida. My mom worked until I was born. She then became a stay-at-home mom who volunteered at my schools. In fact, she did so much for the school system that she was hired as the first paid Volunteer and Business Partnership Coordinator of the Escambia County School System during my school years.

My parents taught me to be kind to others and to live by giving more than you receive. Living by solid principles and values in life was essential. In my younger years, I was shy in school and disciplined to do my work and get along with others. I loved sports and was the first girl to be picked for the sports activities. In fact, I was usually picked in the top 5 selections. That's how I gained popularity in elementary school.

One story stands out in my elementary years. In third grade, my teacher was preparing for a new student. Our desks were connected to make tables. One morning, she put an empty desk by mine. She met with me, letting me know that a new student would be sitting by me. She wanted me to help him as the new student in our class. I was honored with her request. I was excited to meet him and ready to serve. The door opened, and the new student walked in. My heart sank. He was a very heavy boy with a big smile and a sort of gallop in his step. My mind started racing with questions – What would my classmates think about me being this student's buddy? Would they make fun of me as they were making fun of him? At this point, I wasn't seeing this as a special assignment in class. I asked myself, "Why did she do this to me?" I took a deep breath. I remembered that my mom and dad expected me to help others. That's what they taught me. So, that's what I did, and that's what my teacher knew I would do. You see, this young boy needed to know he was valued. Today, I am grateful for my parents teaching me that being respectful, kind, and helpful to others matters. It mattered to the new student, and it mattered to me.

Like many young people, as I moved from middle to high school, life was more about being connected to friends than academics. My middle school friends lived in neighborhoods connected to a different high school than I would attend. On my first day of high school, I went to lunch during fourth period. I realized that I didn't have anyone to eat lunch with. I was humiliated. Over the first week, I found friends to eat with, but it was a rough few days during lunch. When I became a high school math teacher, I promised that I would not let that occur to my fourth period students. For those who didn't have anyone to eat with, I asked them to eat lunch with me, knowing they, too, would find their way.

During my freshman to sophomore year, I made many good friends that I continue to connect with today. Some of my good friends were sitting in that same fourth period class during lunch period. In these adolescent years, I gained energy by pushing the boundaries and valuing creativity, and I became the leader of scheduling fun.

It was at this time that I was introduced to a teacher that paved the path for my future success, Ms. Melrose Coleman. I was a good student and a good athlete, but I was not the best at anything. Somehow, Ms. Coleman saw me as the "best." That's probably the way she saw every student, but, to me, I felt like I was the only one she felt that way about. I took every science course I could from her just to be in her class. I took every opportunity I could to stay after school and talk with her. She always had time for me. Even when I pushed the envelope beyond acceptable boundaries, she didn't judge me. She greeted me with her beautiful smile and small laugh that was so distinguishable. That type of laugh let me know I was pushing the limits. She reached me with love and care.

After graduating from college and working in business and industry for a couple of years, I completed my credentials to become a teacher. I moved back to Pensacola. There was a mathematics teaching position open at this same high school where I graduated. I received the job, and I was reconnected with Ms. Coleman. In fact, my room was right across the hall from her room. To this day, I wonder if she had something to do with that. Is it a coincidence that I was a math teacher teaching on the science wing?

At this point, I was in my early 20s, and I believe the 20s are the most difficult time in life. Ms. Coleman was there for me time and again helping me learn how to navigate life. She listened to me, she guided me without judgment, and she loved me as if I were one of her children. She was my rock.

Ms. Coleman was the wife of a preacher, and she deeply loved her two daughters, Roseanne and Sherry, who were several years older than me. Roseanne and Sherry have lived a spiritual path grounded in their parents' faith. Like them, my values always remained steadfast from my parents' teachings and support. Yet, my path veered in various directions. I often wondered why Ms. Coleman took an interest in me. I took up too much of her time and energy with little return for her. She was truly an angel sent from heaven.

Finally, my path started to straighten. I completed my master's degree and then was accepted into a doctoral program in measurement and evaluation at Florida State University where I received financial support and a graduate assistantship. Ms. Coleman saw me complete my doctoral degree and gain a faculty position at The University of West Florida in Pensacola. She was proud of me. Soon, I didn't have the daily connections with Ms. Coleman that I once had. In many ways, she gave me the wings to fly, and I did. When I saw her, it always brightened my day.

Ms. Coleman was diagnosed with cancer and survived for several years. In 1999, she passed away from a hard-fought battle at the age of 67. I was 35. I saw her in her final days continue to fight for her daughters and her husband. When I walked out of her hospital room the last time I saw her, I knew my job was to fight for all that is right and good that she showed the world. I knew that was the least I could do for all that she had given to me.

I hope that I carry her legacy in just a small way. She never saw me become the dean of the college; start an education company that is grounded in providing the best services to others; and live life with purpose, touching people so they know they matter.

Without Ms. Coleman's influence in my life, I may not have had an opportunity to learn from Quint, write this book and other books, and have an opportunity to dedicate my lifework to leadership.

The greatest gift her daughters gave me is asking me to speak at a celebration of life ceremony for Ms. Coleman. I've never forgotten that time, place, and moment. Ms. Coleman was an extraordinary gift to me.

THANK YOU NOTE

Dear Ms. Coleman in heaven,

You are my Amazing Grace.

How sweet you are,

Who saved someone like me.

You helped me see

That I am valued and

I add value to others.

With your love and deep care,

You set me free to fly.

I love you so very much. You are my extraordinary gift in life.

I am grateful,

Janet

Janet Pilcher

Chapter 2
The Story of Mr. Walter Gulley

I've had the pleasure of being connected to Mr. Walter Gulley in our Pensacola community over the years. Most recently, he and I worked on a community project to save a historical home from being torn down. The home was owned by Ella L. Jordan. Mrs. Jordan dedicated her life to community education and activities and had a rich history of serving families and children at a time when the African American communities did not have access to educational and community resources. The house, now The Ella L. Jordan African American Women's Museum, is a historical place to preserve and offer community education and services while honoring African American Women of Distinction in the Pensacola community.

Mr. Gulley and I were brought together by Ms. Georgia Blackmon, a friend and mentor to me. On September 18, 2023, Ms. Blackmon passed away at 82 years old. Ms. Blackmon was an advocate for children and the black community. She and her husband of 59 years, Johnnie Blackmon, were community educators. Both assumed the role of saving the Ella Jordan Home after it was severely damaged by Hurricane Ivan in 2004.

Mr. Gulley and I were recruited by Ms. Blackmon to help save the home. We were not only willing; we were passionate about the challenge. That's what brought the two of us together. The four of us led the way to raise the money to save the home that is now a beautiful place of educational history. Today, Mr. Gulley is the President of the Board, and I am the Vice President. As we design programs, I am in awe of Mr. Gulley's former students who attend or perform in the programs. They have the deepest respect and regard for him.

In this chapter, I focus on the story told by Monica Woods, a successful business professional who credits Mr. Gulley with paving a path to her future achievements. The theme that ran through my interview with Monica is the phrase, "You can, and you will." She said that's what Mr. Walter Gulley always told us, and those five words still ring loudly in her mind as she hears his resonating voice…a voice that resonated respect, confidence, kindness, and love.

He demanded the best from his students. She claims they delivered because he gave students his best. He pushed students to stretch their minds and abilities. She further suggested, "In stretching our minds, we learned beyond boundaries. In his classroom, we talked about the 'hard' stuff, and I can remember seeing the world differently as I learned from him. Because of his teaching, suddenly what was black and white became so colorful. That understanding of a colorful world has sustained me long into adulthood."

For Monica, Mr. Gulley was larger than life, and he saw something in her that she didn't see in herself; he saw a young mind that needed to be fed encouragement, opportunities, and challenges so she could grow in ways she never imagined.

Mr. Gulley was Monica's high school history teacher. She claimed he was more than a teacher, though. He was her mentor and cheerleader. In her words, "Mr. Gulley is a remarkable man that taught by example, and, to this day, I still reach for my phone to call him when I need to hear that resonating voice of encouragement because he is still my mentor and my friend."

Here's more from Monica on the life teachings of Mr. Gulley.

> Mr. Gulley taught me that I have a voice and that my voice is important. He taught me that there will be times when people or circumstances will try to make you feel small but that I should never, never play small. He taught me that there are times when you are challenged from every angle; your existence is challenged, and what you know is challenged and questioned. In those times, I fall back on what he taught me and what he still teaches me. In that same resonating voice, he tells me, you can do this as "this" is where you come from. "This" is what runs through your veins. He proclaims, "You can, and you will." As an example, he invited me to participate in a Brain Bowl team while I was his student, and he pushed those of us on that team. He possessed a million-dollar smile and a fabulous sense of humor, but in that moment of competition, his message was "Don't smile. It's all about business." But thanks to that "business," we won the Brain Bowl, and every one of us on the team received a college scholarship.
>
> I once heard someone say, "In order to be great, you must make others greater." Mr. Gulley lived that truth. He saw the greatness in each of us. He showed up for us, not just in the classroom, but beyond high school, beyond the expected. The most important truth about Mr. Gulley is he loved us. He loved his students. He also loved his community. And in that love, he taught us the

> value of a spirit of service. He has dedicated his life to his students and the community. And, for that, I say "thank you."

Interviewing Monica about the difference Mr. Gulley made and continues to make in her life is a gift to me. His reach to many students like Monica is worth telling. They live knowing "they can, and they will." I now know that it is this approach to life that called Ms. Blackmon to recruit Mr. Gulley to save the Jordan home. She knew he could, and he did. And, as leaders on the board, together we will serve this home with honor and glory.

THANK YOU NOTE

Dear Mr. Gulley,

Thank you for having a profound impact on Monica as a young mind and as a grown professional. Thank you for always showing up for her and reminding her who she is and the strength and potential she holds. Thank you for teaching Monica to be different and to see the world differently. Thank you for giving her the confidence to spread her wings to fly to places she never dreamed possible. Monica says you fanned the wind under her wings as a young person. Because of that, she is the person she is today.

Because of you, she continues to face every day with "I can, and I will."

With Our Deepest Appreciation and Gratitude,

Janet & Quint

Janet Pilcher and Quint Studer

Chapter 3
The Story of Ms. Myrtice Copeland

The story of Ms. Myrtice Copeland is written by Dr. Charlotte Boling, one of our leader coaches at Studer Education. Dr. Boling is one of the most talented and brightest people I've worked with in my life. I had the pleasure of seeing her grow and develop as a faculty member and leader at The University of West Florida. Dr. Boling left the university to go back into a school district. She started teaching fourth grade and soon became a reading specialist and district leader.

When Charlotte retired from the district, we enthusiastically recruited her to be a member of our team. I am grateful for the many contributions she makes to our team and to our profession.

Hear Charlotte's powerful story that has carried her to where she is today – making a difference in the lives of so many.

Here's Charlotte's story:

It was early September, and Mrs. Copeland called me to her desk. My Language Arts paper was in front of her with a 67 circled in red. In her hand was a pencil – one end blue and the other red. She tapped the 67 with the red end of the pencil as she looked at me. "Charlotte, I know things are sad at your house, but you are a smart girl. I can't have this," she said.

Two years prior, my father had passed away tragically, and there was a huge hole in my heart. The second-grade overachiever was nowhere to be found. My scores flatlined, and it was hard to pay attention. My home seemed empty, school was isolating, and the work was hard. I began my fifth-grade year by walking down to the third-grade hall for reading lessons; it was my walk of shame.

After the meeting at her desk, Mrs. Copeland re-taught the Language Arts lesson and let me try again. I made no mistakes on my second try. Eyeing me carefully, she said, “I’ll make a deal with you. If you give me your very best, you can do your reading lessons with me.” Well, I read every story, did every workbook page, and passed every test in the reading books for third and fourth grades before Christmas break. After Christmas break, she let me continue working at my pace and added frequent trips to the “treasure box” for treats. By the end of the year, I completed the reading curriculum for fifth, sixth and seventh grades. Mrs. Copeland believed in me and created a plan for my academic success.

More importantly, Mrs. Copeland helped me heal. One cold day in February on the way to recess, Mrs. Copeland asked me to recall something about my father that made me smile. It took a few minutes, and then I said, “My dad was a really good whistler.” Mrs. Copeland smiled, making me wonder if “whistler” was a real word. “What did he whistle?” she asked. “You are my sunshine,” I replied. “Today at recess, I want you to find a spot and whistle that song as loudly as you can.” With cold hands in my coat pockets, I remember walking around a tree, whistling as loudly as I could. When recess was over, Mrs. Copeland walked down the line of students, stopped by me, and said, “I believe your dad would be proud of you, and he would really like the way you whistled today.” It was the first time in two years that anyone had talked with me about my father.

Mrs. Copeland changed the trajectory of my life. First, she recognized that I had abilities and needed an opportunity to grow. She put academic expectations in place and held fast to those requirements. Second, she recognized my pain and need for connection. She offered ways for me to express myself and connect with sweet memories of my dad.

Chances are that Mrs. Copeland called every student to her desk and had life-changing conversations with each one. I'm not sure. What I do know is that I am in a different place because of what she saw in that sad fifth grader. Myrtice T. Copeland is my hero.

THANK YOU NOTE

Dear Ms. Copeland,

You are Charlotte's sunshine...you made her happy when skies were grey... you'll never know how much she loves you.

What we know, though, Ms. Copeland, is that you loved Charlotte because you showed her, and she felt it. In a time when she needed someone to see past her low performance to the true potential hidden behind her grief, you stepped up, and you stepped in. You taught Charlotte to be strong and see her own potential despite the circumstances, a lesson she still holds on to today. You taught Charlotte to love reading, and, as a result, she made it her job for many years to teach K-12 reading teachers how to do the same for their students.

Thank you for seeing her potential and not settling for anything less than her best. Thank you for being her sunshine in a dark time and for helping Charlotte find her own sunshine again. In your memory, we see every day how Charlotte continues to shine her light on others.

With Our Deepest Appreciation and Gratitude,

Janet & Quint

Janet Pilcher and Quint Studer

Chapter 4
The Story of Ms. Enga McLendon

Years ago, Dr. KK Owen was presenting what we call a "Connect to Purpose" at a team session. It's a way to connect our work to our purpose by telling a story that reminds us why we do the work we do and serve others. Dr. Owen told the story of Ms. Enga McLendon. As I was asking about possible stories for this book, one of our other coaches, Dr. Gayle Juneau-Butler, remembered the story that Dr. Owen told our team. Together, they worked to offer this story for others to appreciate and learn from. I tell it with the greatest honor of Ms. Enga McLendon.

The love of parents and the commitment and compassion of educators and leaders – that's what brought together a mighty team that fought together to change the world for one young man. Zach is an extreme Type 1 diabetic, and, as a child, his condition was difficult to manage, which resulted in him facing challenges in his school environment. His parents desperately wished he could have a more "normal" educational experience. That hope became a reality with the help of an extraordinary teacher and leader.

Ms. Enga McLendon, a first-grade teacher, had a daughter, Lorna, who like Zach, was born with Type 1 diabetes. During a summer camp for diabetic students, Ms. McLendon met Zach and his parents. She understood all too well the challenges Zach experienced and faced. In fact, Ms. McLendon and her husband wanted the same "normal" school experience for Lorna that Zach's parents wanted for him.

Ms. McLendon encouraged Zach and his family to reach out to KK Owen at N.B. Cook Elementary (Lorna's school) to ask for consideration for their son to be a student there. KK enthusiastically wanted to support Zach, so she convinced her colleagues and the Superintendent to create a loving, safe, comfortable space for him. Zach soon became part of the N.B. Cook Elementary School community. The team of family members, educators, and leaders rallied behind Zach and Lorna to fight for the traditional educational pathway they desired; they continued to fight together as obstacles arose.

Zach continued to thrive throughout elementary school, but sadly, his mother was diagnosed with ALS and passed away when he was in middle school. Adding to the tragic circumstances, his father perished in an accident after his mother died. It's unimaginable what Zach was experiencing. However, because of giving and loving adults, his life path had a chance.

Ms. McLendon and her husband and Zach's parents made an agreement: if anything happened to either couple, the other couple would adopt the children. When Zach lost his parents, Ms. McLendon and her husband upheld their promise, and they became parents to Zach and his sister. Lorna gained a new brother. Ms. McLendon's family grew in number and love.

From the classroom to the living room, this family has continued to overcome challenges together and grow together. Zach and Lorna have since graduated from high school. They did so by engaging in a traditional classroom thanks to passionate parents and educators who persisted with love and care. Zach and Lorna live life with opportunities because of the loving care of a teacher (and mother), an administrator, and a school community. One broken link in that chain would not have afforded Zach and Lorna the educational pathway they experienced.

This is a story of love, sacrifice, persistence, dedication, and giving. It's a story about humankind and people working together to give opportunities to children in challenging situations. It's a story of a teacher, Ms. McLendon, and her family, who assumed the parenting role of a student in need. It's a story of deep commitment and going beyond anyone's expectations to support children who cannot travel life alone. Finally, it's a story of courage to push the boundaries to act in ways that make a difference in the lives of others.

THANK YOU NOTE

Dear Ms. McLendon,

You love fiercely, fight courageously, and believe endlessly.

Thank you for your example that showed us all how to do what seems to be impossible. Your actions teach us how to think differently for the sake of young lives, minds, and hearts. Thank you for challenging boundaries for the sake of embracing the needs of young people. The work you do in shaping young lives is steeped in love. Most of all, thank you for being selfless to save the life of a child.

With Our Deepest Appreciation and Gratitude,

Janet & Quint

Janet Pilcher and Quint Studer

Chapter 5
The Story of Ms. Erin Brodzeller

Sometimes we are called to travel a specific path rather than simply traveling a random path we select for ourselves. That is the story that Dr. Pat Greco tells about Ms. Brodzeller. It's a story that a superintendent shares about a teacher who has a tremendous impact on students and a community. Dr. Greco interviewed Ms. Brodzeller and shares her story and journey that continues to include the lives of her former students.

Ms. Brodzeller's journey into teaching began with youthful idealism, a 22-year-old with a high school English degree and an almost evangelical belief in the power of words. She loved how literature shaped her, how it could unlock empathy and understanding. She wanted to share that magic with her students. For eight years, Ms. Brodzeller poured her heart into her teaching. She also discovered a deep connection with the struggling kids who actively resisted reading and writing. It was those moments of breaking through their tough exteriors, witnessing a flicker of hope in their eyes, that ignited her passion. I hear her say these words, "My heart beat strongest for the students who felt the least connected to school."

Then came a personal pause, the beautiful chaos of motherhood. Ms. Brodzeller took a year away and then received an unexpected call asking if she would consider teaching English to incarcerated 17- and 18-year-old boys at the Milwaukee County House of Correction. She accepted. It was a stark departure from a typical English class. Many of these young men couldn't read. The experience was profound. It shattered any preconceived notions she held and solidified her conviction that literacy is not just a skill, but a fundamental key to opportunity and self-worth for every child.

This experience paved the way for another pivotal moment: the chance to revamp the alternative high school program for The School District of Menomonee Falls in Wisconsin. Here, Ms. Brodzeller was given the freedom to think outside the box to dismantle outdated structures and design experiences that were truly impactful for students who hadn't thrived in the traditional high school setting. It wasn't about adhering to rigid curricula; it was about building relationships, understanding individual needs, and celebrating small victories. She treasured the simple joy of seeing a student finally read a whole book, something each thought impossible. Finding the right books (high-interest and on reading level) finally allowed reading to "click" with the students. She realized it was less about English teaching methods and more about reading as a tool to develop real connections with youth. This connection is best described in her own words: "Students know when you genuinely care, when you truly want to be there for them. That genuine care makes all the difference."

Ms. Brodzeller claims she learned from the best. Her mother was a gifted special education teacher for Milwaukee Public Schools. She professes that her mother modeled the profound satisfaction of witnessing personal student growth, no matter how incremental. Each day, Ms. Brodzeller applies what she saw in her mother. In her work, she feels an igniting of her passion through the enduring connections and success with her students. Years after graduation, she says her students still reach out. In fact, she shares, "A former student, now a barber, cuts my family's hair. Another helped drywall my basement. These are adults I deeply respect. They have lived lives most of us will never have to struggle through. They are my heroes."

Ms. Brodzeller realizes that the evidence of impact that she celebrates isn't what most people would consider grand, but achieving one thing is life-changing for her students and is worthy of celebration.

Listen to some stories in her own words:

> We had two girls arrive at high school with zero credits and a deep-seated aversion to school. Within two weeks of being in our alternative program, they felt success for the first time. Their parents, noticing the shift, called to ensure their children were truly okay. These students were thriving, even enrolling in a trade school. They sent me screenshots of their improved grades, a testament to their newfound confidence. Of course, not every story has a happy ending. Some students face significant challenges, and legal troubles may persist. But I try to stay connected to offer a glimmer of hope even in the darkest of circumstances. One former student, after five years in prison, is now at Milwaukee Area Technical College, working toward a better future. Seeing his resilience is a powerful affirmation.
>
> We celebrate the little goals: working for 15 minutes straight, something that felt insurmountable in their previous school environment. We make a big deal out of small achievements, offering a hug at the door or allowing them to take a walk to clear their heads. These simple acts build trust and demonstrate that they are capable of hard things. Reading a book from cover to cover, especially for students who have spent years faking understanding, is a monumental achievement.

> One student remains etched in my heart and memory. He came to our alternative program while on Huber release from the Milwaukee County Jail, and he was still wearing his orange jumpsuit and ankle bracelet on a gun charge. I had known him in middle school. His father had recently passed away. It was a profound loss he carried with him every day, but he came to our school daily. His mother cared deeply. Her son found a connection with me. He wrote papers, and he had the time and space to read. No one expected him to succeed, yet he graduated. He got off probation and started at the lowest level of work for a luxury home builder. The owner recognized his potential and mentored him. Today, he is a master carpenter, and I hire him for projects around my house.
>
> The depth of our connection was truly revealed when he attended my husband's funeral, coming alone, without friends, simply to offer his support. That selfless act, that quiet demonstration of care, resonated deeply and solidified the profound impact these students have on me just as much as I hope to have on them. My passion for teaching isn't just about imparting knowledge; it's about fostering real human connection, believing in potential, and witnessing the beautiful, messy, and ultimately triumphant unfolding of individual lives.

As an educator for many decades, Dr. Greco has witnessed many excellent teachers. She chose to share the story of Ms. Brodzeller in this book. It represents the deepest form of human connection that truly saves students' lives, especially those in some of the most vulnerable situations.

THANK YOU NOTE

Dear Ms. Brodzeller,

Sometimes, life takes us on a wonderful journey, and we simply enjoy the ride and the stops along the way. Your journey has taken you into the lives and hearts of students who have often been considered "hard to reach." But you have always stopped for them. You stopped and made them feel valued, loved, and worthy. You stopped to show them how to learn and how to love learning not because they had to but because they could. You tore down walls and built bridges in lives, and you showed young lives that learning is more than books and classrooms; it's about life and relationships, and it's about the journey.

Thank you for going to the hard places in students' lives and for allowing them to go to the hard places in life with you. We need teachers like you in education to make our world a better place.

With Our Deepest Appreciation and Gratitude,

Janet & Quint

Janet Pilcher and Quint Studer

Chapter 6
The Story of Ms. Robbie Fackelman

I had an opportunity to listen to the interview that Dr. Greco facilitated with Ms. Robbie Fackelman. Sometimes we hope writing people's stories does justice to the impact those stories had on someone's life. Ms. Fackelman didn't see anything special about what she did as a teacher. Teachers are called to care for their students, and that's exactly what Ms. Fackelman did during her tenure as a teacher. Sometimes we start a journey down a path and then take a detour to what we are called to do. That is Ms. Fackleman's story, and it's a story worth telling.

For Ms. Fackelman, the path to the classroom was unexpected. She graduated from college with a mathematics degree, intending to join the business world. Teaching or nursing was the expected path for women at the time; however, she declared, "That is not what I'm going to do." Life sent subtle nudges. She was asked to be a Teaching Assistant, and she found she was a natural at helping others learn. Rather than staying on the path to an MBA, she enrolled in a few education courses to complete the certification requirements to teach.

Ms. Fackelman's early teaching experiences were at a diverse school in the south. She discovered a deep connection with the students and a genuine love for the intricacies of mathematics. Her passion for her work with students intensified when she transitioned to West Bend, Wisconsin. Teaching, she says, was a decision that she "wouldn't change." Teaching fueled her personal desire to change lives.

Ms. Fackelman's passion for math was kindled by her own experience with a high school math teacher, who navigated his classroom from a wheelchair. This teacher believed in Ms. Fackelman's potential and introduced her to advanced mathematical concepts like calculus. He instilled a crucial sense of confidence. Half of the students in her college calculus class dropped within weeks of the semester starting, but thanks to Ms. Fackelman's early experiences and the confidence her high school teacher fostered, she thrived. The profound influence of her high school math teacher shaped her academic success and, more importantly, her self-belief.

This experience was a cornerstone of Ms. Fackelman's own teaching philosophy. She recognized the anxieties many students, particularly girls, harbored towards mathematics. Their self-doubt often stemmed from negative learning experiences coupled with a lack of encouragement. Comments from students, such as "I liked math until 7th grade when I learned I'm not good at math," fueled Ms. Fackelman's determination to counter the typical narrative. She wanted to grow the confidence students often lacked. She actively engaged with their work on tests and quizzes, offering personalized feedback and alternative approaches. Her aim was to demystify the subject and reveal its inherent beauty. Ms. Fackelman's goal was to ensure her students not only grasped mathematical concepts but also felt capable in their learning. She celebrated the success stories, like a former student who later became an engineer and attributed his confidence to her early encouragement.

Ms. Fackelman's passion was further fueled by observing other effective educators. She loved the ability to see the moments when genuine understanding illuminated a student's face. She found immense satisfaction in guiding students toward their clarity. Ms. Fackelman maintained high expectations, and she understood her role in showing students "how to get there." She loved it when students shared real-world examples of geometry, and she remembered a German foreign exchange student writing back to her, sharing that he tutored his peers in math after his return home. Seeing her students pursue fields reliant on mathematics, like pharmacy, reinforced the lasting impact.

Ms. Fackelman knew she had true impact when she saw an enlightening shift in her students' confidence. She saw their growth as they tackled unfamiliar problems, exhibiting a willingness to try new approaches. She built trust in her relationships and demonstrated a belief that each student was truly capablo.

Ms. Fackelman shared the true impact of seemingly small gestures. She once received a letter from a student years after he graduated. The student shared how he became a chemist and had a growing family. He shared in the letter to Ms. Fackelman that he suffered from severe depression during high school. He let her know that her simple greetings each day and the personal care she took with him made him feel seen and valued. Ms. Fackelman didn't know his personal struggles at the time. Rather, she saw him as a quiet young man with a lot of potential. His message underscored the profound, and often unseen, impact teachers have on students' lives. Each year of her career, Ms. Fackelman wrote personalized letters to her graduating seniors. This student's message deepened the significance of her personal touch. Each connection, no matter how small, was a tangible expression of her belief in them.

For Ms. Fackelman, the unexpected journey into teaching became her calling, a living testament to the power of connection, the impact of an early mentor, and the profound satisfaction of growing strength in others. Her story is not simply about teaching mathematics. It is about making a tangible difference in the lives of her students, one equation, one encouraging word, one heartfelt letter at a time.

THANK YOU NOTE

Dear Ms. Fackelman,

You have demonstrated the perfect equation: love and care + motivation and encouragement + math concepts and principles = a highly impactful math teacher.

Thank you for balancing the equation in the lives of so many and inspiring a love of a subject often feared. Thank you for patiently and lovingly seeing each student as a mind with potential and the ability to be "good at math." You showed so many young people, particularly young women, that math is approachable and conquerable. Thank you for teaching them to have confidence in themselves and their abilities by having confidence in them; you shined a light on the potential they often couldn't see. Thank you for responding to life's nudges and listening to the inner call to go where your heart led you – into the classroom.

Because of you, lives were changed, and because of those changed lives, the world has been exponentially changed.

With Our Deepest Appreciation and Gratitude,

Janet & Quint

Janet Pilcher and Quint Studer

Chapter 7
The Story of Ms. Tiana Walker

I've had an opportunity to connect to an outstanding Pre-K teacher through one of our retired leader coaches, Dr. Robin Largue. When Dr. Largue retired, she wanted to select one thing to commit to doing. After a year, she made that selection. She joined a program in her local school district and became a Pre-K "reading pal." Every year, she is assigned a student to mentor. She recently completed her second year and has become a dedicated volunteer at C.A. Weis Elementary School in Pensacola, Florida. That is where she met Ms. Tiana Walker, an incredible person and educator.

I've been connected to C.A. Weis Elementary School in different ways over the years starting from my time as a faculty member and dean of the College of Professional Studies at The University of West Florida. Also, one of our leader coaches, Dr. KK Owen, was a principal at the school decades ago. Today's principal, Dr. Kim Thomas, is one of my doctoral graduates. She is a shining star. She hires and supports excellent teachers like Ms. Walker.

C.A. Weis is a school located in a high-poverty neighborhood. Over 90% of their students receive assistance due to economic disadvantage. Ms. Walker loves teaching at Weis so that she can support students and families that need to be cared for and served well.

I had an opportunity to interview Ms. Walker. Soon into the interview, Ms. Walker described her feelings about being a

Pre-K teacher: "It's my calling. It's my home." Indeed, she is right at home with her "babies" in her classroom at C.A. Weis Elementary, and they are at home with her. Her high energy and passion for her work exudes the love, tenderness, and care that water the seeds in young hearts and minds. As her young students buzz around the classroom, they hang on every word of the gifted educator who guides them.

Ms. Walker has been teaching at the elementary-school level for 10 years, and most of that time has been in Pre-K classrooms. She admits to feeling a true sense of calling and joy in teaching young children, but truth be told, she's more to her students than a teacher. She's a friend, counselor, mentor, social worker, and so much more. She gives a voice to her students as they learn to use their own voices. She offers them a solid foundation at a young age to be successful in life.

She helps her students feel safe, and she creates an atmosphere that supports those feelings. In fact, her goal is to develop what she calls a "safe haven" for all students. Ms. Walker understands that her students may not have that kind of environment elsewhere in their lives. It's not uncommon for parents of her former students to request her to be the teacher for one of their other children. The parents see the impact Ms. Walker can make, and the parents want that for all their children.

Ms. Walker finds great joy in being part of a child's first educational experience. She thrives on the thrill of seeing them write their names for the first time, advance their social skills, learn how to interact and communicate, make friends, and gain confidence in themselves. She commits to giving every student a positive first educational experience, offering them every opportunity for continued success. She is driven by this commitment from day one until the time that they “graduate” from her class and enter kindergarten. As I continued to talk to Ms. Walker, I thought how lucky every child would be to have a Ms. Walker at age four.

Ms. Walker’s efforts don’t stop with her students. She is committed to the families and communities that her students come from; she meets each of them “where they are” even when that means taking on extra work for herself. Ms. Walker claims, “It’s worth giving extra time and effort. My students’ and families’ growth and successes pay it back to me. When you build that strong bond with the students and their families, there's a sense of purpose and being, and you know you're doing the job. You know you’re where you belong.” Ms. Walker certainly belongs in the classroom. She ensures that her students and their families matter in life – that they are valued and important.

As a testament to this fact, Ms. Walker once had a student for whom English was not her first language. In fact, at this time, the student couldn’t speak English at all – not even one word – nor could her family. Ms. Walker worked hard to communicate with both the student and her family (often finding people to help translate for them), and she embraced the hard work of teaching the student despite the language barrier. Ms. Walker tackled the situation by fully investing herself in helping the student do the hard work of learning a new language and managing in a class where the student did not understand what was being communicated. Because of Ms. Walker, this student came to class with an eagerness to learn, and her parents were committed to her daily attendance. Thanks to Ms. Walker, they never gave up on learning.

At the end of the school year, the student spoke her first clear words to Ms. Walker in English: “I love you.” Those three words have never been more powerful to Ms. Walker as they were that day. Yes, the student had been trying to learn single words in English throughout the year, but it was a challenge to understand her. That day, though, in perfect English, she clearly said those three words, and she meant them because she knew Ms. Walker loved her back. Thanks to Ms. Walker's love and commitment, the student pushed through despite her language barrier.

Several years later, Ms. Walker was blessed to have this student's younger cousin as a student. Because she had built strong relationships with the student's family previously, they were all sprinting out of the gate from the first day of school to see success for the younger cousin. What a powerful example of Ms. Walker's impact on young lives and minds. Ms. Walker is a master at building relationships with students and their families.

Every year, Ms. Walker closes the school year with her class celebration. This celebration is similar to graduation, and it marks a milestone in her students' educational journeys. It's an opportunity to highlight and celebrate what the students have learned, how much they have grown, and how they have demonstrated success. It's an opportunity for the families and teachers to continue to build relationships as they collectively celebrate the children they all love. Together, they laugh and cry during the picture slideshow Ms. Walker has so lovingly prepared, cheer as the children stand on stage to sing songs they've learned, and simply celebrate the growth of young lives. Ms. Walker says, "I can always count on one thing. Every parent wants the best for their child. My responsibility is to give them my best so they can be their best."

Ms. Walker displays a current picture of each child in a picture frame, much like a senior portrait. She then gives each student a "ring pop" for their class rings. At the end of the ceremony, she gives the pictures to their families, asking them to keep them to place alongside their child's high school graduation photo in the future. She purposely positions this graduation experience to set the stage and expectation for her students, encouraging them to graduate and pursue successful, happy lives. Graduating from Pre-K highlights future possibilities.

Why does she invest so much in her work? Because "It's her calling. It's her home." She says that teaching Pre-K children reminds her to appreciate the small things in life, to uphold the little joys, and to pay tribute to the precious curiosities in life. Her young students remind her to be flexible and to nurture the sparks of curiosity and the small interests that can grow like wildfires if fanned. Her ultimate goals, though, are to lay a positive, solid foundation for a strong educational future and to teach her students to be good humans. And we can all agree that Ms. Walker is not only a good teacher; she is also a good human.

THANK YOU NOTE

Dear Ms. Walker,

Thank you for accepting your calling and for building your home big enough for so many young lives. Thank you for making a place for others to belong and for showing love and speaking love in every language. Thank you for giving and being "so much more" to your students and their families. Thank you for being a good human and growing good humans. We have found in you a kindred spirit because we share the same DNA, the DNA of one who loves and believes in education.

Today, we celebrate you and your commitment. May your calling always ring loudly in your ears and may your "home" continue to grow each year as new students grace your classroom walls.

With Our Deepest Appreciation and Gratitude,

Janet & Quint

Janet Pilcher and Quint Studer

Chapter 8
The Story of Principal Jeannie Clark and Ms. Laressa Finney

In our coaching work, we are fortunate to work with Douglas School District in Box Elder, South Dakota, where Mr. Kevin Case is the Superintendent of Schools. Dr. Casey Blochowiak, one of our leadership coaches, shared a newspaper article with me, showcasing a recognition program at Francis Case Elementary School. After reading the article, I interviewed the principal and teacher connected to the story. The principal, Ms. Jeannie Clark, read my book, *Hardwiring Excellence in Education*. As the district worked with Dr. Blochowiak to apply the tools and tactics from the book, Ms. Clark decided to start by focusing on Chapter 9. That chapter provides approaches aligned with Principle 9: Reward and Recognition. In essence, Ms. Clark led her school to bring Principle 9 to life.

I interviewed Ms. Clark and the second-grade teacher, Ms. Laressa Finney, highlighted in the news article. Their story is powerful, and I am honored to tell it.

Teachers touch our lives in so many ways, and we are forever grateful for our teachers. But how often do we tell them how much they are appreciated and the impact they have on young lives? The magnitude of this question led Principal Clark to start a gratitude program at Francis Case Elementary School, and the result has been a change in the school culture. As the principal, she loves being able to work with students and adults, and the gratitude program has impacted the lives of those connected to the school.

Principal Clark recognizes that gratitude is easy and incredibly powerful, yet it's not something we automatically do. We often think that demonstrations of appreciation must be big. In practice, however, Principal Clark notes that small gestures of appreciation have significantly boosted school morale, which is evident in daily interactions. She recognizes how the teachers and staff have grown closer together as they nurture relationships through appreciation of one another. The impact of this appreciation extends further, cascading to how students interact with each other. Principal Clark states, "The small things are a reminder to every single person that their efforts are seen and valued."

Second-grade teacher, Ms. Laressa Finney, joined the interview with Principal Clark. Ms. Finney began her teaching career at Francis Case Elementary School and is completing her tenth year. Principal Clark noted how Ms. Finney continues to grow and thrive in her classroom. Principal Clark elaborates, "Ms. Finney is committed and willing to jump in when I suggest something new, so her response was to jump in and participate when I began our gratitude program. It has had a profound impact on her and her classroom."

In true teacher form, Ms. Finney is focused on her students and being her best for them. To Ms. Finney, receiving thank you notes as part of the gratitude program has enhanced her ability to give her best and be her best for her students. Sure, it feels good to her when she receives a note of appreciation. In fact, Ms. Finney expresses that the gratitude notes significantly impact how she feels about herself. They affirm something great within her that is being recognized by others.

Ms. Finney also shares that she learns from the messages in the notes, using the information to identify specific actions that are appreciated. This helps her understand what she needs to continue doing to achieve excellence. In Ms. Finney's own words, she states, "As educators, we are always striving to do better and be better. When I personally receive a note, it helps me know what to keep doing in my classroom with my students." She also emphasizes that notes of gratitude boost morale and build connections among teachers, creating an environment where everyone can bring their successes and strengths to the table for acknowledgement and celebration. Ms. Finney believes this builds a sense of camaraderie among teachers, and students ultimately benefit.

If you walk into Ms. Finney's room, you'll see a wall decorated with notes and tokens of appreciation. She admits that these demonstrations of appreciation instill feelings in her of being needed and valued, and these feelings create a ripple effect that even students feel.

Principal Clark and Ms. Finney proudly speak about the impact the recognition program has on students, noting that "giving thank you notes rubs off on students." When their students see adults giving notes of appreciation to each other, they begin voluntary recognizing fellow students.

As students began following what they observed the adults doing, they followed suit, recognizing each other. Ms. Finney feels the joy from this shift, observing students sharing notes with one another. For example, she recalls one student who wrote a thank you note to a peer who had helped him with a challenging math problem. Now, Ms. Finney encourages students to use notes to thank each other, cementing this practice as part of their classroom culture.

In addition to being a teacher at Francis Case, Ms. Finney is also a Francis Case parent; her twins recently completed first grade there. Ms. Finney mentioned that one of her twins struggled in school this past year. As is customary for first graders, he participated in a visit to the second-grade classes in preparation for promotion to second grade. His mother's classroom was naturally on his tour because she is a second-grade teacher. Inspired by the positive example Ms. Finney set, one of her students wrote her son a note of advice with tips for second grade. This thoughtful gesture from her student to her child beautifully illustrates the care the student has for Ms. Finney. Driven by his care and concern for his teacher, he extended care and concern to her son. We often say that writing thank you notes is contagious, and this unsolicited act of kindness shows just that. The interactions among the adults effectively taught students how to care for, respect, and appreciate others.

We can learn a lot from our students when we watch and listen. I believe that young people crave positive interactions with adults and with their peers as much as adults desire positive interactions. Ms. Finney is masterful at creating an atmosphere for these interactions to ignite and multiply.

Principal Clark noted that through this type of interaction, she realizes the value the notes can have with parents. In fact, she will expand the recognition approaches to parents during the next school year. Ms. Finney shares, "From a teacher's perspective, it's incredible to see what the demonstrations of gratitude do for the school, but experiencing it from a parent's perspective helps me understand how to be more empathetic with parents. Being both a teacher and parent, I can see it from both perspectives."

Every year, we work with Douglas School District to administer and roll out the results of a parent survey. One of the lowest-scoring items on that survey pertains to parents receiving positive feedback about their child. By using gratitude notes with parents, Principal Clark believes they can improve in this area. It's simply the next layer of building a culture of gratitude.

Principal Clark also has a way of displaying the notes she receives. She explains, "I have my own wall of notes and demonstrations of appreciation like Ms. Finney because they feed my soul. Students come in my office and ask me about them, and I proudly explain what they are and their significance. They need to know that appreciation feels good for us all."

I asked her if there was a specific time with a student that stood out to her. She responded, "One of my favorite notes was from a student who was moving from our school, and the transition was painful for him. Before his move, he brought me a note and told me to wait until he left my office to read it. Once he left, I carefully opened the note and read "I love yoe," which means "I love *you*." And he signed his name. Not long after that, he asked me if I liked his note...if he only knew." That story is one that refuels the passion for Principal Clark. It's an interaction she will never forget.

Leaders, teachers, and staff at Francis Case know that it's important to intentionally express appreciation to each other by using a note of thanks to recognize people. As they demonstrate, doing so has a profound impact on others. We all want to be seen. We all want to be appreciated. We all want to be valued. And we all want to show how we add value. That's what those working at Francis Case Elementary School do every day with each other and their students. Small acts of kindness make a big difference in the way people feel about themselves and each other.

THANK YOU NOTE

Dear Principal Clark and Ms. Finney,

When we developed Principle 9: Reward and Recognition as one of the Nine Principles, we never imagined seeing this principle come to life as it has at Francis Case Elementary School. Principal Clark – thank you for the courage and creativity for making recognition and gratitude a part of your school culture. We hope that every school leader learns from you and is inspired to do the same.

Ms. Finney, as we heard about your acts of gratitude and kindness in your classroom, we quickly realized you don't know just how great you are. That's what most teachers do, isn't it? Go to school, teach, love their students, and expect little in return. With this note, we say a HUGE thank you for being a teacher. Your students and their families are lucky you chose this awesome profession.

With Our Deepest Appreciation and Gratitude,

Janet & Quint

Janet Pilcher and Quint Studer

Chapter 9
Expressing Gratitude for the Extraordinary Gift

The stories we tell in this book are only a tiny fraction of the stories being lived yet not often told. Quint and I hope this book inspires us all to intentionally express our gratitude to teachers, staff, and leaders. To support you in doing just that, we share this chapter, which focuses on ways to express our appreciation for teachers and staff. When we express appreciation, we show we care for others. We show people they are valued and how they add value to the lives of others.

When people are appreciated, they feel that others care for them as individuals. When people are recognized, they feel that their work matters. They tend to feel better about themselves and are energized to continue to give their best.

To effectively show this care and recognition, we intentionally look for the bright spots, make the good become visible to others, and express our appreciation with specific words that show a person's value.

One way we coach leaders to connect with their employees is by having rounding conversations with them. Rounding conversations are intentional, one-on-one conversations with employees to learn more about who they are, what they care about, how leaders can be helpful, what's working well for employees, and where they are getting stuck. Rounding conversations also include questions that ask employees about who has been especially helpful to them and what they did to be helpful. The answers to these questions provide leaders with opportunities to appreciate people, resulting in a win-win-win situation. The person receiving the recognition feels good about themselves. They also feel good about the person who recognized them and the one giving the recognition. Never underestimate the difference appreciating others can make. A small, seemingly simple act touches someone's life in a memorable way.

We leave you with three simple yet powerful ways to appreciate people who come to work making a difference in the lives of students and families.

1. **Continue to tell stories like the ones you read in this book.** You can easily capture these stories by starting meetings or the day with a story that connects us to our purpose. Ask people to share a story about a teacher, staff member, student, parent, or leader – or any others whose kind act made a difference in their lives.

2. **Create a space for bright spots and words of thanks.** Make that part of your workspace and communicate why this space exists and how people can contribute.

3. **Write thank you notes to express your appreciation to others.** Let people know they are valued and show them how they add value. Be specific with your words. The details are important.

We can't thank people enough. Let's do it often and with great intention. Pay attention to all the good that is going on, jot it down, and express appreciation. By doing so, we create ripples in a pond. One pebble thrown in a pond creates one ripple that multiplies to many ripples that are far reaching in a short period of time. Like a pebble in a pond, stories of appreciation inspire others to continue the gift of giving. Expressing gratitude becomes contagious.

One of our greatest contributions to our profession can be telling stories about people who make a difference in the lives of others. These stories are unfolding every day. We hope this book is a catalyst for bringing untold stories to life.

What is your story? Who has made a difference in your life? How did they value you and show how you add value to others? The final chapter of this book offers a space for you to write your story about someone who made a difference in your life. Close the story with a note of appreciation. Then present them with that gift of your words of appreciation.

To our teachers, you are the extraordinary gift of life. This book could be never-ending, full of stories about how you made others' lives worthwhile. You do make a difference, and you teach us to make a difference in the lives of others. This book is our gift to you.

You matter. Thank you.

With Our Deepest Appreciation and Gratitude to
The Extraordinary Gift: Our Teachers,

Janet and Quint

Chapter 10
Share Your Story of an Extraordinary Teacher

We have left this chapter of the book blank for you to use. Dedicate a few minutes of time to honor an extraordinary teacher that impacted your life. If you feel so inclined, don't hesitate to send them a handwritten thank you note to share your appreciation and thanks.

Teacher's Name:

Create Your Story and Thank You Note:

About the Authors

Janet K. Pilcher, Ph.D

Janet is the founder and president of Studer Education. She has an extensive background advising educational institutions on strategic planning, leadership development, employee engagement and operational improvement. Janet and her team work with education leaders to elevate their organizations into places where people have purpose, do worthwhile work, and make a difference.

Before moving into consulting, Janet spent nearly 20 years at The University of West Florida (UWF) as a professor, associate dean and dean of the College of Education and Professional Studies. There, she received and oversaw $17 million of grant and contract projects and achieved one of UWF's research distinction awards. While at UWF, Janet co-created TeacherReady, an online teacher certification program that prepares second-career teachers worldwide. She also started an education entrepreneurial center focused on developing assessment and feedback strategies to improve systems and classrooms.

She is the author of several books, book chapters, and research articles. Janet's most recent book, *Hardwiring Excellence in Education*, has touched the hands of over 10,000 educators to date. She is also the host of the podcast, *Accelerate Your Performance*, sharing high-performing leadership practices and leveraging the great leadership and systems improvement work of education executive leaders throughout the country.

Quint Studer

Quint Studer is a lifelong student of leadership. He has a gift for translating complex strategies into doable behaviors that allow organizations to achieve long-term success.

Quint is a best-selling author of leadership books that have influenced leaders throughout the country. He has authored 16 books, presented his work at healthcare and professional conferences throughout the world, and is a renowned speaker.

Quint started his professional life as a special education teacher before transitioning to healthcare. He served in executive positions, building leadership capabilities to achieve high-performing outcomes for patient experience. He served as the President of Baptist Hospital in Pensacola, Florida, initiating their journey to achieve the Malcolm Baldrige Award. From there, he founded a healthcare consulting company, Studer Group, a high-performing leadership coaching organization. He led that organization to be a recipient of the Malcolm Baldrige Award in 2010. Working with Dr. Janet Pilcher, he provided the groundwork to begin Studer Education to transfer the best practices in healthcare leadership to education leadership.

In his most recent venture, Quint founded Healthcare Plus Solutions Group (HPSG) with a mission of having a positive impact on those who receive care and those who provide care. He also started a nonprofit organization, the Studer Community Institute. A key initiative of the institute, the Building Brains Program, is designed to give every child the opportunity to be the best they can be and move the needle on kindergarten readiness. Quint is a passionate leader who continues to make a difference in healthcare, education, and our communities.

About Studer Education

Studer Education partners with education leaders to improve student outcomes by strengthening the people, processes, and structures that power educational systems. Our dedicated team of coaches deliver measurable, lasting improvements in leadership, operations, and student achievement. Every partnership is grounded in data and focused on outcomes—because we don't just advise, we work alongside education leaders to hardwire excellence.

The Studer Education Leadership Framework™ is an evidence-based approach designed to improve organizational performance by building capacity, empowering people, and creating an action-driven environment that monitors progress and accelerates results. It focuses on aligning organizational goals, behaviors, and processes to support the core mission of providing high quality education.

Connect with a Studer Education team member to discover how to hardwire excellence in your educational system.

- Call: 1-800-259-3105
- Email: info@studereducation.com

Visit us online: www.StuderEducation.com

Resources to Continue Your Learning

Hear More Stories of Gratitude on the "Accelerate Your Performance" podcast. While this book empowers teachers directly, the Accelerate Your Performance podcast extends the conversation to education leaders. When you listen, you'll gain insights on thriving educational environments and inspiring stories that celebrate the powerful work occurring in education. Join us to hear how leaders are championing educators and their efforts.

https://studereducation.com/accelerate-your-performance-podcast/

Other Books to Complement *The Extraordinary Gift*

- Pilcher, J. (2023). *Hardwiring excellence in education*. Huron Consulting Services, LLC.
- Studer, Q., & Pilcher, J. (2015). *Maximize performance*. Fire Starter Publishing.
- Studer, Q. (2023). *Sundays with Quint*. Gratitude Group Publishing.
- Studer, Q. (2012). *The great employee handbook.* Fire Starter Publishing.